**GREAT ENGINEERING**

BUILDING
BRIDGES

REBECCA STEFOFF

 Cavendish Square

New York

Published in 2016 by Cavendish Square Publishing, LLC
243 5th Avenue, Suite 136, New York, NY 10016

Library of Congress Cataloging-in-Publication Data

Stefoff, Rebecca, 1951- author.
Building bridges / Rebecca Stefoff.
pages cm. — (Great engineering)
Includes bibliographical references and index.
ISBN 978-1-50260-598-6 (hardcover) ISBN 978-1-50260-597-9 (paperback)
ISBN 978-1-50260-599-3 (ebook)
1. Bridges—Juvenile literature. 2. Bridges—Design and construction—Juvenile literature.
3. Civil engineering—Juvenile literature. I. Title.

TG148.S74 2016
624.2—dc23

2014046859

Editorial Director: David McNamara
Editor: Andrew Coddington
Copy Editor: Rebecca Rohan
Art Director: Jeffrey Talbot
Designer: Amy Greenan
Senior Production Manager: Jennifer Ryder-Talbot
Production Editor: Renni Johnson
Photo Research: J8 Media

The photographs in this book are used by permission and through the courtesy of: My Leap Year/Shutterstock, cover; File: José Luis Mieza/Wikimedia Commons, 5; B2M Productions/Image Bank/Getty Images, 7; UbjsP/Shutterstock, 8; Walter Quirtmair/Shutterstock, 9; Kimson/Shutterstock, 11; Chris Sattlberger/Photographer's Choice/Getty Images, 12; Jeremy Bright/Robert Harding World Imagery/Getty Images, 13; Auremar/Shutterstock, 15; Robert Cernohlavek/Shutterstock, 17; World History Archive/Newscom, 18; drpnncpptak/Shutterstock, 20–21; J.K. Floyd/Shutterstock, 23; Hulton Archive/Getty Images, 24; Ventdusud/Shutterstock, 26.

Printed in the United States of America

TABLE OF CONTENTS

CHAPTER **ONE**: From One Side to the Other Side   4

CHAPTER **TWO**: Making a Plan   10

CHAPTER **THREE**: Building the Bridge   16

CHAPTER **FOUR**: A Better Way Across   22

Glossary   28

Find Out More   30

Index   31

About the Author   32

CHAPTER ONE

From One Side to the Other Side

Some of the world's biggest cities are near water.

New York City has more people than any other American city. It is built around two rivers. They flow into an ocean harbor.

Paris is the biggest city in France. It has a river running through it. So does London, the biggest city in England.

There's one big problem with rivers. How do you get to the other side?

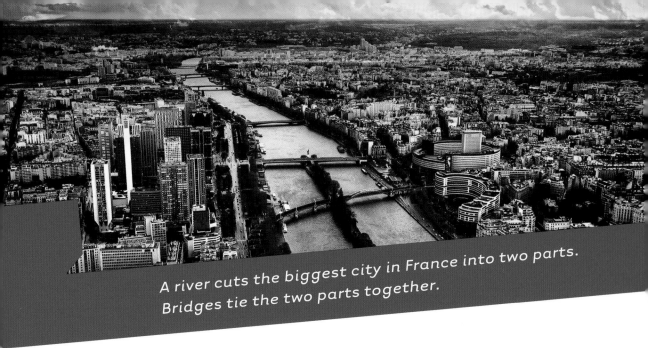

A river cuts the biggest city in France into two parts. Bridges tie the two parts together.

The Wet Way Across

The first people moved around looking for food. They had to cross creeks and streams to find food on the other side. Those people splashed their way through the water to get to the other side.

Wading through the water is one way to cross a creek. Swimming is another way. But what if the water is icy cold? That could keep you from wading or swimming.

The flow of the water could stop you, too. Water flow or movement is called **current**. If the current is fast, you could get swept away.

What if the water is deep and wide? You might be able to walk across a creek. You might swim across a stream. But a river might be too deep to walk across. It might be too wide to swim across. You need another way to get to the **opposite** side.

A New Way

Imagine you want to cross a creek. How would you start? You would look up and down the creek banks for the best place to cross.

Not far away you see a tree that has fallen down. Its trunk lies across the creek. One end of the trunk is on your side. The other end is on the opposite side of the creek.

The tree is big enough to walk on. It looks better

The world's first bridge was probably a log over a stream.

than trying to walk or swim through the water.

You carefully walk along the fallen tree. It takes you to the other side of the creek. You have just used a **bridge**.

A bridge goes from one side to the other side of something. Most bridges are over water. They cross creeks, rivers, and lakes. Some bridges go over busy streets so people can walk safely across.

Bridges can also cross **canyons**. A canyon is a valley with steep sides—like the Grand Canyon. Often there is a river at the bottom of the canyon.

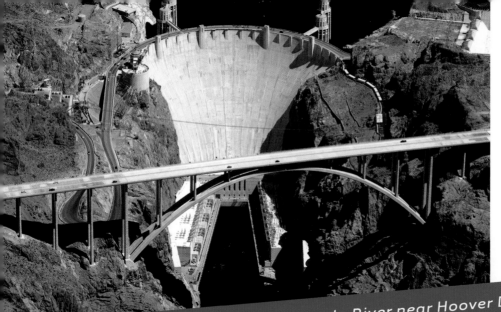

This bridge spans the Colorado River near Hoover Dam. It links two states, Arizona and Nevada.

Making Bridges

The first bridges that people made were simple. Suppose there was no fallen tree across a creek. People just cut down a tree to make a bridge.

People still make bridges by putting a log or a board across a small creek. This is the easiest kind of bridge to build. But a board is not big enough to cross a river.

The distance that a bridge has to cross is called its **span**. People had to learn to build bridges that could span rivers or valleys. The ancient Romans built bridges with blocks of stone. Some of their bridges are still in use today. They are about two thousand years old.

Today, big, new bridges are made of metal. They have to be strong. They carry many people, cars, trucks, and trains every day.

Simple bridges made of rope and boards are still used in many places.

CHAPTER TWO

Making a Plan

There are three main reasons to build a bridge.

Old bridges can wear out. An old bridge can be dangerous. If it starts to wear out it may **collapse**, or fall down. Sometimes it is easier to build a new bridge than fix an old one.

More people and cars. When the number of people goes up, a city may need more bridges. In 1887, the city of Portland, Oregon, had one bridge across its river. Portland kept growing. Now it has eleven bridges.

People want an easier way. The countries Denmark and Sweden are on opposite sides of a

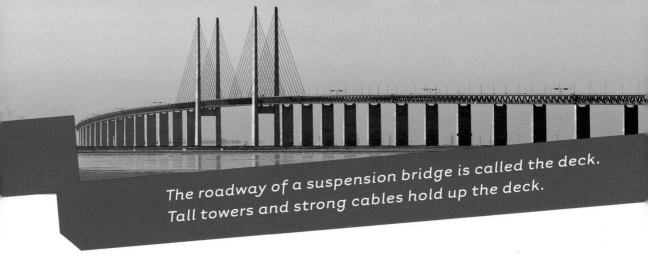

The roadway of a suspension bridge is called the deck. Tall towers and strong cables hold up the deck.

narrow strip of sea. For a long time, only boats or airplanes could go from one country to the other. Then the two countries built a bridge. Now cars, trucks, and trains can go back and forth.

Building a bridge starts with a plan. Making a plan starts with **engineers**.

Engineers and Engineering

Engineers are makers. They use the tools of science to get things done. Their work is called **engineering**.

There are many kinds of engineers. They figure out how people can make all kinds of things, from cars to computers. The engineers who work on

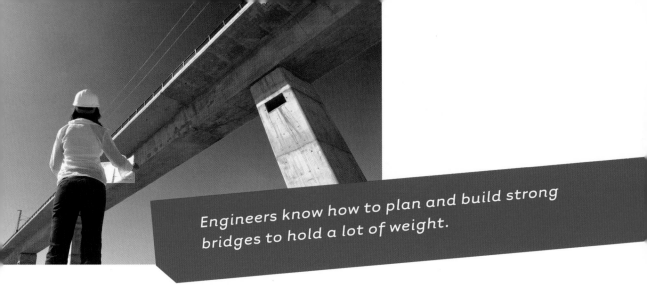

Engineers know how to plan and build strong bridges to hold a lot of weight.

bridges, dams, highways, and other public works are called **civil engineers**.

Engineering is very important when building a bridge. Engineers know about materials, such as steel and **concrete**. For example, they know how thick a steel **cable**—or rope—has to be to hold up a bridge.

Engineers also know how materials react in different types of weather. For example, when it is cold out, concrete shrinks—or gets a little smaller. When it is hot out, concrete expands—or gets a little larger. An engineer knows how to plan for this.

The Three Kinds of Bridges

There are three main kinds of bridges. An engineer has to pick the right kind for the place where the bridge will be built.

Beam bridges. The simplest bridge is the beam bridge. Remember that fallen tree over the creek? That was a beam bridge.

A beam bridge is flat and straight. The part that crosses the span is called the beam. Modern beam bridges are held up by thick posts at each end and sometimes in the middle. This kind of bridge is good for short spans.

Arch bridges. The old Roman bridges are arch bridges. This kind of bridge can cross longer spans than beam bridges.

This arch bridge in Rome was built more than two thousand years ago.

An arch bridge curves upward in the middle. That makes it strong. The weight of the bridge presses outward toward the ends.

Suspension bridges. For the longest spans, suspension bridges are used. A suspension bridge is held in place by huge slabs of concrete buried in the ground at each end.

Big cables run between the concrete slabs. Towers on land or in the water hold up the heavy cables. Smaller cables run down from the big cables. The smaller cables carry the deck—the part of the bridge where people and cars cross.

It Takes a Team

Engineers alone do not plan bridges. Most bridges today are big jobs that cost a lot of money. Many people help plan them.

Some of those people study the land where the

bridge will stand. Can it hold the weight of the bridge?

Other people study traffic, meaning the flow of people and cars. How many of them will use the bridge? It has to be big and strong enough to hold them.

Other people study the weather. Will the bridge have to stand up to high winds? What about ice or burning heat?

Finally, the engineer draws a plan. This shows all parts of the bridge, from the largest to the smallest. The plan will tell the builders where and how to do everything. The engineer might also make a small model to show how the bridge will look.

Now the bridge can be built.

Building the Bridge

Building a bridge today can be a big job. It might take hundreds of people. Work on a long bridge can last for years.

The two ends of the bridge are built first. Then the workers build from the ends to the middle. Good engineering is needed. The parts have to meet perfectly in the middle.

Working in Water

Building a bridge means working in water. Most

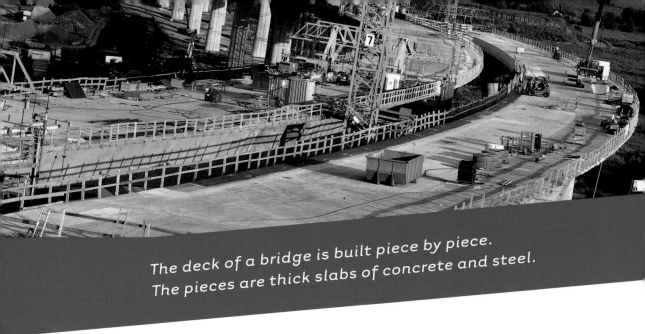

The deck of a bridge is built piece by piece. The pieces are thick slabs of concrete and steel.

bridges have posts or towers that rise out of the water. How are those towers built?

Engineers have two tools for building underwater. They are the **caisson** and the **cofferdam**.

Both the caisson and the cofferdam are big boxes that are watertight. This means that water cannot leak into them. They are closed on top but open on the bottom.

A caisson or cofferdam is lowered into the water until it rests on the bottom. Then a pump pushes the

STEEL CAISSON.

water out and fills the box with air. People can now work on the river bottom, inside the box.

As the workers dig, the box sinks lower and lower. When the box reaches solid rock, the digging is done. If the box is a caisson, it is filled with concrete. A tower built on top of the caisson will help hold up the bridge.

A cofferdam does not stay on the river bottom. It does not become part of the bridge. Cofferdams are used to give workers a safe, dry way to work in water. When the work is done, the cofferdam is taken away.

Handling Heavy Loads

People today can still build a simple bridge with rope, wood, and a shovel. But building bigger bridges means moving heavy material. Engineers plan to use machinery.

A bridge is not built from scratch on the place where it will stand. Instead, the main pieces of the bridge are made in factories. Trains or large trucks carry the pieces to the building site.

At the site, bulldozers and earthmovers shape the land. A bridge is not the only thing that has to be built. The engineers and workers also have to build roadways so that people can get on and off the bridge.

Flat boats called barges carry caissons and cofferdams out into the river. The barges have

The tall metal tower is a crane. It can lift heavy loads, like the concrete pieces of a bridge.

BUILDING **BRIDGES**

special machines called cranes. The cranes lift the caissons and cofferdams. Then they lower them into the water.

Taller cranes called tower cranes lift huge pieces of the bridge into the sky. Then the crane driver slowly lowers each piece into the right place.

The deck of the bridge is made in sections. Each section has long pieces of steel covered with concrete. The center section goes in last. When it is in place, the bridge is done. People can now walk or drive across it.

CHAPTER FOUR

A Better Way Across

Pioneers who crossed the country to settle in the American West traveled a hard road. For some, the hardest part was crossing the Snake River.

The Snake River winds through Idaho and Washington. For much of the way, it lies at the bottom of a tall canyon. Pioneers had to lower their wagons and animals down the steep canyon walls. Then they chose the best place to cross the river. After that, they

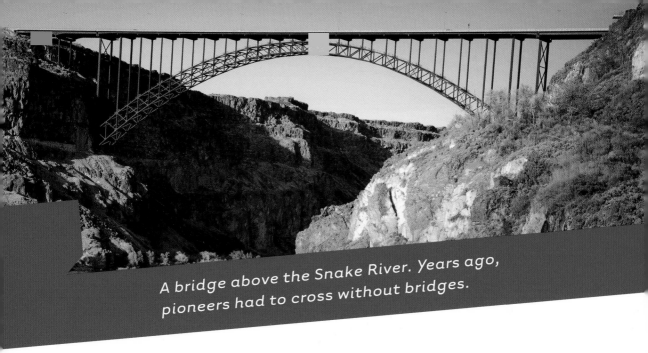

A bridge above the Snake River. Years ago, pioneers had to cross without bridges.

had to climb up the other side of the canyon.

Many pioneers lost their wagons in the Snake River Canyon. Some lost their lives. Today, dozens of bridges cross the canyon. People can drive safely and quickly over the Snake River.

All over the world, bridges make life easier for people. Two of the most famous bridges in America were built to solve big traffic problems.

The Brooklyn Bridge opened in 1883. People set off fireworks to celebrate.

Brooklyn's Big Bridge

The Brooklyn Bridge in New York City took fourteen years to build. The bridge spans the East River between two boroughs, or parts of the city, called Manhattan and Brooklyn.

Before the bridge, the East River was jammed with boats. They carried people and goods between the two parts of the city. Storms made the water rough. Winter turned it to ice. People wanted an easier, safer way to get around.

The Brooklyn Bridge was an engineering wonder. When it was built, it was the longest suspension bridge in the world. On the day the bridge opened, more than 150,000 people and 1,800 cars crossed it!

Bridging the Bay

San Francisco also needed a bridge. The city sits on a point of land surrounded on three sides by water. As the city grew, people built homes across the water. Every day, thousands of people had to go from their homes to their jobs in the city—and then back home again.

From the city, there were two ways to reach the towns on the other side of San Francisco Bay. One was to drive around the bay. It was a long drive that took

many hours. The other way was to cross on a boat.
Waiting in line to get on a boat could also take hours.

Finally, in 1933, the city started building a bridge
across the bay. It took four years. The suspension
bridge went from San Francisco to a point of land

just opposite the city. It swooped over the entrance to the bay.

That entrance was called the Golden Gate. The bridge was given the same name. The bridge is not gold, though. It is painted dark orange. People around the world know the Golden Gate Bridge by its special color.

Almost thirty-nine million cars cross the Golden Gate Bridge each year. People can walk across it, too. Its main span is 4,200 feet (1,280 meters) long. Bridges have come a long way since the days of logs across creeks!

GLOSSARY

arch bridge A bridge supported by one or more arches, shapes that curve upward in the middle.

beam bridge A bridge that is a flat surface (the beam) held up by thick posts; good for short spans.

bridge Something that crosses a gap or an open space, such as a river or canyon, and connects the two sides.

cable A thick, heavy rope made of up many thinner lines twisted together; made of steel in large modern bridges.

caisson A structure like a big box that is sunk into water and becomes the base of a tower.

canyon A valley with steep sides, usually with a river at the bottom like the Grand Canyon.

civil engineer An engineer who makes bridges, dams, roads, and other structures for the public to use.

cofferdam A structure like a big box that is sunk into water; the water is pushed out so that work can take place inside the cofferdam; after the work, the cofferdam is taken away.

collapse To fall down or break apart.

concrete A blend of sand, gravel, cement, and water that is hard and strong when it dries.

current The flow of water, or the speed at which the water is moving.

engineer Someone who uses science to plan and create things.

engineering The work of engineers.

opposite Across from, or on the other side of, something.

span The open space that is crossed by the bridge; a bridge is said to have a span, or to span a gap.

suspension bridge A bridge that hangs by cables from towers that are anchored to the ground.

FIND OUT MORE

Books

Hoena, Blake, and Angie Kaelberer. *Building the Golden Gate Bridge: An Interactive Engineering Adventure*. Minneapolis: Capstone Press, 2014.

Latham, Donna. Bridges and *Tunnels: Investigate Feats of Engineering*. White River Junction, VT: Nomad Press, 2012.

Squire, Anne O. *Extreme Bridges*. Minneapolis: Children's Press, 2014.

Websites

10 of the World's Longest Bridges

www.cnn.com/2014/04/15/travel/worlds-longest-bridges

Building Big: All About Bridges

www.pbs.org/wgbh/buildingbig/bridge/index.html

INDEX

Page numbers in **boldface** are illustrations. Entries in **boldface** are glossary terms.

barges, 19
boroughs, 24
bridge, 7
    arch bridge, **13**, 14
    beam bridge, 13
    suspension bridge,
        14, 25, 26
Brooklyn Bridge, **24**, 25

cable, 12, 14
caisson, 17–19, 21
canyon, 7, 22–23
civil engineer, 12
cofferdam, 17–19, 21

collapse, 10
concrete, 12, 14, 18, 21
cranes, **20**, 21
current, 6

deck, **11**, 14, 21

engineer, 11–17, 19
engineering, 11–12, 16, 25

Golden Gate Bridge, **26**, 27

Hoover Dam, **8**

opposite, 6

Snake River Bridge, **23**
span, 9, 13, 14, 24, 27

ABOUT THE AUTHOR

Rebecca Stefoff has written books for young readers on many topics in science, technology, and history. She is the author of the six-volume series *Is It Science?* (Cavendish Square, 2014) and the four-volume series *Animal Behavior Revealed* (Cavendish Square, 2014). She also wrote *The Telephone*, *The Camera*, *Submarines*, *The Microscope and Telescope*, and *Robots* for Cavendish Square's Great Inventions series. Stefoff lives in Portland, Oregon, sometimes called "Bridgetown" for the many bridges that link the two halves of the city together across the Willamette River. You can learn more about Stefoff and her books for young people at www.rebeccastefoff.com.